With love:
To Alexander Strait
from
Grandma Elsa

CONQUEROR
AND
HERO
THE SEARCH
FOR ALEXANDER

CONQUEROR
AND
HERO

THE SEARCH
FOR ALEXANDER

STEPHEN KRENSKY

DRAWINGS BY ALEXANDER FARQUHARSON

LITTLE, BROWN AND COMPANY
BOSTON   TORONTO

FIRST EDITION

Library of Congress Cataloging in Publication Data

Krensky, Stephen.
   Conqueror and hero.

   Summary: Outlines the life of Alexander, a
charismatic individual who was simultaneously the
king of Macedonia, pharaoh of Egypt, and emperor of
Persia.
   1. Alexander, the Great, 356–323 B.C. — Juvenile
literature. 2. Greece — Kings and rulers — Biography
— Juvenile literature. [1. Alexander, the Great,
356–323 B.C. 2. Kings, queens, rulers, etc.]
I. Title. II. Title: Search for Alexander.
DF234.K83   938′.07′0924   [B]   [92]   81-3791
ISBN 0-316-50373-8   AACR2
ISBN 0-316-50374-6 (pbk.)

BP

*Published simultaneously in Canada
by Little, Brown & Company (Canada) Limited*

PRINTED IN THE UNITED STATES OF AMERICA

For Phyllis Wender

FOREWORD

The life of Alexander the Great was a spectacular one. And like all impressive lives, his inspired love, hate, admiration, jealousy, and fear. In the twenty-three hundred years since his death in 323 B.C., the emotions surrounding Alexander's life have clouded the facts. Who Alexander was, what he did, and why he did it are questions still argued about today. Answering them completely is difficult; we have no complete accounts of Alexander's life written by anyone who actually knew him. The major existing sources were compiled more than three hundred years after his death. Of these, the most vivid is Plutarch's and the most accurate is probably Arrian's. It is from Plutarch that I have drawn the quotations used here. These two Greeks drew on older books that no longer exist. This lack of solid information left me to make some educated guesses about my subject. I have reconstructed Alexander's life using events from different sources that are most consistent with one another and the period. I have also included some of the legends about Alexander, stories that reveal both aspects of his nature and the way other people viewed him. Distinguishing the facts from the fiction was a difficult task. To do a more subtle sifting would take a finer sieve than I could find.

CONQUEROR
AND
HERO
THE SEARCH
FOR ALEXANDER

ILLYRIA

EPIROS

MACEDONIA

Strymon
Nestos

THRACE

BLACK SEA

Loudias
Axios
Amphipolis
Mt. Pangaion
Philippi
Kavalla
Komotini
Mesemvria
Edessa
Yannitsa
Pella
Derveni
Abdera
Lefkadia
Nikesiani
THASOS
Veroia
Sedes
Stagiera
Vergina (Aigai)
Thessalonike
SAMOTHRACE
Tsotyli
Kozani
Pydna
Dion
Olynthos
Madytos
Vitsa
Haliakmon
Mt. Olympos
Potidaia
CHALKIDIKE
Ilion
Hellespont
Tempe
Homolion
Mt. Ossa
AEOLIA
MYSIA
Pelinnaion
Larissa
Volos
Demetrias
THESSALY
LESBOS
Myrina
Kyme
Karditsa
(Palaiokastro)
PHTHIOTIS
EUBOEA
Sardis
AEGEAN SEA
Delphi
Eretria
CHIOS
Thebes
ATHENS
Ephesos
Magnesia
Corinth
SAMOS
IONIA
PELOPONNESOS
Olympia
Argos
DELOS
Messene
Sparta
KOS
Rhodes
IONIAN
SEA
RHODES
Lindos
CRETE

Cyzicus

The Greek World
with Archaeological Sites
of Ancient Macedonia

0   40   80   120   200 KILOMETERS
0   20 40   80   120 STATUTE MILES

Sam. H. Bryant

1

The world of Alexander the Great, over twenty-four hundred years ago, was a much simpler place than the world is today. Most people were farmers, craftsmen, or soldiers. Their jobs took up the bulk of their time. Few of them could read or write, and many never left the towns where they were born. Their possessions were basic and functional. Common Greek clothing was a rectangular piece of cloth with a hole for the left arm, pinned on the right shoulder and along the right side. Houses were made of sun-dried brick. There was no glass for windows. The fastest communications went by horseback, signal fire, or sailing ship. Wars were frequent, and conquered people were usually killed or enslaved.

Though details of life varied from place to place, the basic pattern did not. Physical survival was the main order of business, and few survived without a struggle. Around the Mediterranean Sea, the lands that we now call the Cradle of Western Civilization rocked almost constantly with war. The centuries had witnessed the rise and fall of the Egyptian and Babylonian empires, among others. The Greek peoples, including Alexander's ancestors, played no part in this earlier history, however, for they had not yet settled in the region.

The Greek migration only took place several hundred years before Alexander's birth. The Greeks came from the north and found the Mediterranean peninsula an agreeable place. The winters were wet but mild. Snow usually fell only in the mountains. The hot summers were relieved by gentle winds. Though many of the plains were barren, some grains could be grown there. Grape vines and olive trees flourished. The land was not lush enough to support cattle, but goats, sheep, and pigs thrived and multiplied.

The few fertile valleys were far apart, isolated by hilly countryside. The communities founded in those valleys grew to be cities that flourished independently from one another. The land was dotted with these city-states. Each one had its own government, army, laws, and concerns. The Greeks shared a common ancestry, language, and religion, but they fought among themselves for land, trade routes, natural resources, and prestige. Religious observances were almost the only thing that brought the Greeks together peacefully. Even these gatherings, which were athletic festivals, were competitive. The most famous one was the Olympic Games, held every four years in honor of the chief Greek god, Zeus.

The Olympic Games, however, did not contribute to a more widespread peace. For more than one hundred years before Alexander's birth in the middle of the fourth century B.C., the city-states spent a lot of time at war with

4

one another. Once in a while they banded together to fight foreign foes, but only when the mutual threat was too great to ignore.

The two most prominent of the feuding city-states were Athens and Sparta. Athens was a democracy, where citizens voted for their laws and their leaders. It was the home of a rich culture of literature, art, music, and philosophy. Sparta was a monarchy; power there was held by only a few men. It was a soldier-state where discipline and toughness were more important than cultural pursuits. These different outlooks caused a constant irritation between the two powers, one they could not resolve in peace. Athens and Sparta each had a time of supremacy among the city-states, yet through pride and misfortune each also squandered its chance to unify Greece.

The city-states were busy enough fighting among themselves to stay clear of many armed conflicts with the northern kingdoms that shared their peninsula. They would support rival tribes and pretenders to various thrones, hoping such mischief would keep the northern kingdoms weak, but that was all they did. Kingdoms such as Illyria and Thrace were not even peopled by Greeks, and so the city-states, with their notions of Greek superiority, had little use for them.

Macedonia was different. Most of its natives were not Greek either, but Greek blood did course through the veins of the royal family. In fact, Macedonian kings claimed descent from the legendary hero Heracles, as impressive an ancestor as any Greek could want. Nevertheless, Greek culture had never been deeply rooted there. The focus of city-state life was the city, and the culture and trade that sprang from it. Macedonia had its cities, of course, but its people were more tribal and rural. Its population was dispersed over the countryside. The north held great natural resources, especially in timber and metals, but its strength had never been asserted on a large scale.

Philip II, who was Alexander's father, was to change all that. When he was born in 382 B.C., Macedonia was not an important kingdom. Unruly nobles jealously guarded their own power. Philip's growth to manhood paralleled the emergence of the city-state Thebes as a major force in Greece. When he was fifteen, he was sent to Thebes as a hostage. The reason for this is unclear. Perhaps it was a way for the Thebans to keep some control over Macedonian affairs. Whatever their motive, their act had far-reaching consequences. During the next three years, Philip received a Greek education while being able to observe closely Greek military strategy and diplomacy.

When Philip was released, he returned to Macedonia. A few years later, his father died. Philip's baby half-brother inherited the throne, but he was too young to rule. Philip was appointed his regent, which meant he would rule until his brother grew old enough. The young regent had a traditional Greek appearance with his curly hair, straight nose, and thick beard. Later battles would leave him lame in one leg and blind in one eye, but at the time his ambition and looks were well matched.

Good looks, though, were not enough to protect a kingdom. Neighboring tribes eyed Macedonia hungrily. They thought an infant king and an inexperienced regent would be easy to swallow up. They were wrong. Philip had learned his military lessons well in Thebes. Marching from foe to foe, he won a string of victories. Naturally, his countrymen were impressed. Here was a leader who should be king, not merely regent. Tradition allowed them to make such a change, and so Philip was elected king over his brother.

The new monarch spent several years making himself supreme in northern Greece and the Balkans. In the process, he reorganized his army. Before Philip, armies didn't practice fighting, they simply fought whenever the need arose. Many battles were lost through lack of experience. Philip made his soldiers train all year round. The army practiced handling weapons and carrying heavy packs on long marches. Philip focused his attention on the phalanx, spearsmen who fought together as a unit of eight to ten rows. Philip closed the distance between their shields and lengthened their spears. Longer spears were awkward to use at first, but once mastered, they were deadly to foes whose spears were only half as long.

Not all of Philip's acquisitions of land were the result of war. He gained the mountainous realm of Epirus by marrying its princess, Olympias. Love was not considered necessary for royal marriages, and it was not included here. From all accounts, Olympias was a willful young woman. Philip had his ambitions and she had hers. Both of them, however, wanted an heir to the throne.

That heir was Alexander. He was born in 356 B.C., the year after the wedding. Philip was not home at the time. News of the birth reached him the same day he won an important battle and his horses won victories at the Olympic Games. Philip took these triumphs to mean that his son

A gold medallion picturing Olympias, Alexander's mother.

was favored by the gods. Certainly the omens were good.

As pleased as he was to be a father, Philip spent little time with his young son. Care of the young prince at first fell to his nurse, Lanice, with his mother always hovering nearby. Olympias' cousin, Leonidas, oversaw Alexander's early education, and it was he who started the prince's military training. Heirs to the throne might expect an easy, pampered life. Alexander was treated differently. Leonidas was determined to make Alexander physically tough, and he did his work well. The hardships Alexander endured prepared him for military life as few boys had ever been prepared.

Other aspects of his education were not ignored, however. Most boys of his time would simply have learned a trade or a craft and little else. Alexander was taught to read and write. He also practiced the art of speaking. A skilled speaker could impress both educated and ignorant people. For a future leader who would someday have to rouse his troops, speaking well was essential. Such leaders also had to fight well. Alexander spent many hours learning to ride, to use a sword and a spear, and to understand military concerns.

The success of this intensive training was evident at an early age. The story is told that when Alexander was six or seven, two Persian governors visited the royal court at Pella. Philip was away fighting so Alexander played host. During meals and other gatherings, he asked his guests many questions about the Persian Empire. What were some of the Persian customs? How fast could the Persian army travel across its vast territory? What were the strategic points of value? The Persians were surprised at these questions. They did not expect such shrewdness from a young boy. When they left Macedonia, news of the clever prince went with them.

The Greeks valued the body as well as the mind, and here too Alexander stood apart. He was striking looking, rather than conventionally handsome, a well-proportioned youth of middle height. His slightly curling blond hair and fair skin were set off by an aquiline nose and dark eyes. Other boys might be taller or broader, but there was something about Alexander's expression that commanded attention and respect.

In addition he possessed notable athletic skills. Alexander was a tireless runner and had great ability as a horseman. He was even encouraged to enter the Olympic Games. This would have been a great honor to anyone else, but it failed to excite him. Athletic contests did not interest Alexander for their own sake. If Alexander was going to risk

A head of Alexander the Great, probably sculpted during the decade after his death.

failure, it would be for a higher goal. "I will enter the Games," he reportedly said, "if the other entrants are of equal rank." They weren't, of course, because the Olympic Games were open to all Greeks. So, true to his word, Alexander did not compete.

The prince had a special chance, though, to display his horsemanship. One day he watched Philip and some friends attempt to break in an expensive horse, Bucephalus. The name means "ox-head." Bucephalus got the name from having either an ox-shaped brand on its flank or a similar natural mark on its head. Whichever, the horse was certainly stubborn as an ox. No one could master the spirited animal. After observing the many failed attempts, Alexander spoke up. He criticized the horse's handlers. Philip reproached him: Did Alexander know more than his elders?

"I could manage this horse," Alexander replied, "better than others do."

"And if you do not," said Philip, "what will you forfeit for your rashness?"

Alexander answered quickly, "I will pay the whole price of the horse." This was a large amount, one that Alexander would spend a long time paying off. Philip accepted the bet; he would teach his rash son a lesson.

The moment was now Alexander's. He approached the horse carefully. Speaking gently in Bucephalus' ear, he grasped the bridle. Alexander had noticed that the horse was skittish about its shadow. And naturally, the more Bucephalus reared, the more frightening its shadow became. When Alexander mounted, he faced Bucephalus directly toward the sun. The horse's shadow stretched out behind them, where Bucephalus couldn't see it. Alexander turned the horse around only after his control was established.

Philip and his friends were amazed. "My son," the king commented, "you must find a kingdom worthy of yourself. Macedonia is too small for you."

Philip's pride was understandable. Alexander had shown boldness and confidence, both important traits for the future. His education had gone well so far; it was time to take a further step. Philip had already surrounded Alexander with royal pages drawn from the nobility. The king hoped to bond the boys in friendship, ending the rivalries that had plagued Macedonia in the past. Now he hired the famous philosopher Aristotle to teach Alexander and the pages. It was Philip's aim to give Alexander the same advantages that he, Philip, had gained in Thebes.

Aristotle stayed in Macedonia for three years. The forty-ish philosopher and the thirteen-year-old prince got along well from the beginning. Aristotle had ideas on almost every subject, ideas reflecting a refined system of logic. He kindled Alexander's interest in philosophy, medicine, and science. Even difficult philosophical ideas intrigued the prince. He enjoyed discussing things few people could understand. Aristotle had much to offer him.

Their study focused on Homer's *Iliad,* the epic poem that recounts the history of the Trojan War. Among its heroes was Achilles, a legendary ancestor of Alexander's on his mother's side. Achilles was the supreme warrior, almost invulnerable in battle, though sensitive in spirit. He was easily offended. This ancient hero greatly attracted Alexander, who wished to surpass his achievements. The *Iliad* also interested Alexander for other reasons. It featured fighting skill, courage, endurance, cleverness, and compassion, all prominent aspects of Alexander's nature. He memorized most of the long poem, and for the rest of his life kept a copy nearby.

The final Greek triumph in the *Iliad* demonstrated to the Greeks their superiority over foreigners. This prejudiced view was one Aristotle, like most Greeks, still held. He tried without success to instill it in Alexander. The young prince thought more broadly than in Greek terms alone. Life in the Macedonian capital of Pella had exposed him to many cultures that had strengths as well as weaknesses. And like Philip, Alexander had a practical nature. He would judge people by their deeds, not their backgrounds.

During the time of Aristotle's teaching, Alexander continued to see much of his mother, but Philip had grown increasingly distant from Olympias. She apparently spent much time with soothsayers and prophets, and joined in strange religious rites. Some of them involved snakes, which she kept in her chambers as pets. Philip was not fond of snakes in a bedroom. In addition, Olympias' arrogance and sour disposition made her even more disagreeable. Philip began looking elsewhere for companionship. Macedonian kings traditionally married often, and Philip already had several wives less important than Olympias. None of them, however, had borne him a son.

Soon Philip married again. His new bride's name was Cleopatra, like the famous queen of Egypt who lived three centuries later. The marriage displeased Olympias. She did not attend the wedding feast, though Alexander was there. The royal banquet was magnificent. The food was served on fancy gold and silver dishes, and wine was drunk from engraved goblets. Dancers and musicians performed for the guests, who thoroughly enjoyed themselves. They were pleased that Philip now had a Macedonian queen, not just foreign ones. Cleopatra's family had the most to celebrate, and her uncle, Attalus, had too much to drink. At one point he called out for the gods to give his niece a lawful successor to the throne. He meant a successor who had only Macedonian blood.

Alexander knew what he meant and he didn't like it. Probably he had not been sharing in the merriment, and this insult was too much for his pride. After all, he was then the lawful heir to the throne. Could Cleopatra claim ancestors equal to Olympias'? Tempers flared on both sides. Philip joined in, blaming Alexander for disrupting the celebration. He would have attacked his son, but he too had drunk a lot of wine, and fell down crossing the room.

"See there," said Alexander, "the man who makes preparations to pass out of Europe into Asia, overturned in passing from one seat to another." Having said that, he wisely departed. Olympias, about to leave for her native home, found him ready to accompany her. He continued on to Illyria, where he spent several months.

Philip's anger with his son cooled as his head cleared. The king and the prince needed each other. Philip wanted a loyal Alexander at his side to show that the Macedonian monarchy was strong and stable. And Alexander wanted Philip's backing in giving him a worthy military command. So the prince returned to Pella.

Yet all was not calm between father and son. Philip had arranged a marriage between his half-witted son, Philip Arrhidaeus, and the daughter of the governor in Caria. Olympias and others convinced Alexander that this marriage would threaten his position. So, he sent an actor to Caria to ask that he, Alexander, be allowed to marry the governor's daughter instead. Clearly Alexander was nervous. Many princes of his time had seen power snatched from their grasp, their lives ending in death or exile. Alexander wasn't against this policy, he simply wanted to be the one in control of it. In this case, his fears were unnecessary. Yet Philip was furious with him. How could Alexander waste himself on such a minor alliance? Was it a fool he was training to be king? The act was unworthy of his trust. In punishment, Philip sent some of Alexander's closest friends into exile.

The rift between father and son remained, but it was

bridged by their mutual ambitions. Philip was finally preparing to attack the city-states. After twenty years of fighting, he had control that reached far beyond the Macedonian borders. Not surprisingly, his military success had already drawn the city-states' attention. From 350 B.C. onward the Athenian orator Demosthenes devoted much of his talent to denouncing Philip's aggressions. He saw Philip wishing to control Greece as Athens had sought to control it a century earlier. But Philip had other ideas. He knew that the history of strife between city-states made governing them as a single country impractical. What Philip wanted was an alliance establishing peace at home so that all the Greeks could fight the Persians together. Naturally, Philip saw himself commanding the Greek force.

Despite the warnings of men like Demosthenes, the city-states had been slow to be stirred against Philip. Their own weaknesses and domestic squabbles got in the way. Besides, the feelings about Macedonia were mixed. Some leaders viewed Philip as a potential ally, not an enemy. With their help, he was steadily drawn into the affairs of southern Greece.

Finally, though, Athens joined with Thebes to confront Philip. A treaty between Philip and the Athenians had existed since 346 B.C., but in the last eight years both sides had ignored its terms whenever they became inconvenient. Philip was now prepared for a showdown. He knew that Athens and Thebes must be defeated to gain his ends.

The crucial battle was fought at Chaeronea in 338 B.C. The opposing forces each numbered around thirty thousand, but Philip's strategic skills and his army's better conditioning gave him the advantage. On the right wing, he had his phalanxes fall back before the Athenian attack. Meanwhile, on the left wing, eighteen-year-old Alexander led the cavalry charge against the Thebans. As the left wing broke through the Theban ranks, the retreating phalanxes turned abruptly and attacked the Athenians. Their retreat had been a trick to draw the Athenians forward and isolate them. They suffered heavy losses and retreated. With Alexander coming from the left, and Philip now attacking from the right, the opposing center crumbled in defeat. Victory went to Macedonia.

Philip could now dictate terms to most of Greece. Even in defeat, though, Athens remained powerful. It was a heavily fortified city that would be difficult to subdue and occupy. Philip still needed Athenian goodwill and their fleet to fight the Persians. So he dealt leniently with them. He was less kind with the Thebans, from whom he needed nothing.

The vanquished city-states sent representatives to Corinth in 337 B.C. to meet with Philip. There he negotiated a treaty among them. The city-states could keep their domestic independence in return for a united foreign policy. Only in Thebes did Philip meddle internally, replacing a hostile government with one more sympathetic to his goals.

The outcome of the treaty was the League of Corinth, the formal association of city-states, kingdoms, and independent tribes of Greece. One of its first acts was to appoint Philip to lead the armed forces. By law, the post would also pass to his heirs. Philip in turn set plans into action for the Persian campaign. His public goals were to free the Greek cities in Asia and to revenge the Persian invasion of Greece 143 years before. Had these reasons not existed, Philip probably would have found others. The Persian Empire was too tempting a prize for him to ignore.

Early in 336 B.C., Philip's general Parmenion led a force into Asia Minor to establish a military base. How successful Philip's campaign there might have been can never be known, for he was assassinated before it properly began. His murderer was Pausanias, a member of his bodyguard. This bitter young man had been embarrassed by Cleopatra's uncle, Attalus, and Philip had done nothing about it. The rumor was that Olympias had encouraged Pausanias to turn his anger toward Philip and had even helped plan the assassination. Certainly she had been angered by Philip's recent marriage, especially now that Cleopatra had given birth to a son. This son might later threaten Alexander's claim to the throne if Philip lived on. Suspicion thus fell on Alexander as well. Nothing was proved, and his participation in the scheme seems unlikely. Alexander took great risks to achieve his goals, but planning his own father's death hardly fitted the heroic tradition he admired.

Whatever really happened, Alexander blamed the Persians for Philip's death. Certainly they benefited from the death of Greece's greatest living general. Whether Alexander actually thought they were guilty, or just wished to protect Olympias, blaming the Persians was useful to him. They could not defend themselves against the accusation, and it gave the Greeks one more deed to avenge.

Philip's death came at the peak of his career. He had risen from obscurity to become the leader of Greece and the Balkans. He had changed the concept of strategic warfare, combining elements of infantry and cavalry that had fought separately before. His training methods also went a long way toward establishing a professional army. Though his debts were large, he had laid the foundation for the Persian campaign and built a framework in the League of Corinth that would serve Alexander well.

2

Alexander was just twenty years old when he became king of Macedonia. There was little time to mourn his father's death. Philip's most important generals, Antipater and Parmenion, supported Alexander, and this gave him control of the army. But strong rivals for the throne remained. Alexander had to prove himself — and quickly. He began by putting these rivals to death, showing himself to be Philip's match in ruthlessness. Not to be outdone, his mother would soon have Cleopatra and her infant son killed, too. It was a grim start to the new reign.

His advisers cautioned Alexander to move slowly. They feared the inexperienced king might lose everything through some rash action. Alexander looked at the situation differently. Philip's death had stirred rebellion in many areas, reflecting a lack of respect for the new king. No one doubted Alexander's bravery, but some might say that his achievements in battle had owed more to Philip's planning than to his own skill. Alexander intended to remove these doubts. He subdued some of the northern tribes on his way to Corinth, where he wanted to be appointed Philip's successor. The League wasn't ready to argue with the Macedonian army, so they confirmed Alexander as commander of the Greeks.

While in Corinth, Alexander visited the philosopher Diogenes, whom he had heard much about. Diogenes was an unusual man. He lived as simply as possible, sometimes wearing a barrel instead of clothes. The tale is told that he once walked through the crowded city at night with a lantern, searching for one honest man. Such a figure intrigued Alexander. He found Diogenes sitting on the ground, thinking. The philosopher did not rise as the king's shadow stretched across him. Alexander introduced himself and offered to grant Diogenes a request. The philosopher had only one — that the king step aside to let the sunshine reach him. Alexander took no offense. While his companions laughed at Diogenes' sour manner, Alexander admired him for his steadfast beliefs. Supposedly, he even said, "Were I not Alexander, I would wish to be Diogenes."

Though officially in command, Alexander still had revolts to settle. He snuffed them out like a string of flickering candles. One notable victory came against a large group of Thracians. They controlled a mountain peak, with great wagons ready to roll down on any attacking foes. This did not stop Alexander. As the wagons rumbled down the narrow mountain passes, he had his soldiers lie on the ground beneath their shields. The wagons then rolled harmlessly over them. Their defense gone, the Thracians quickly surrendered.

Farther north, Alexander confronted a large tribe of

Celts at the Danube River. The Celts were mostly gathered on the far side, but some of them had taken up posts on an island in the middle of the water. Alexander sent his few ships against the island, but the strong current and small numbers hindered the attack. While the Celts enjoyed Alexander's discomfort, he reconsidered his position. Moving upstream, he captured every small boat he could find. He also had his men stuff their tents with hay and tie up the ends, so they could be used as rafts. Then, in one night, he ordered the whole army across the Danube in the small boats and makeshift rafts. They surprised the Celts, who could not imagine that Alexander would have any way of reaching them. The Celts fell back before the Macedonian attack in amazement. A treaty was soon arranged, one that lasted for the next sixty years.

As successful as Alexander was, the fighting nevertheless took months. While he was busy in the north, a rumor spread over southern Greece that Alexander had died in combat. This wishful thinking caused fresh revolts, especially in Thebes.

The political exiles had returned to Thebes, replacing the rulers Philip had installed. The Thebans had already revolted once since Philip's death, but Alexander had pardoned this first offense. Now they were revolting again.

Alexander rode south as soon as the news reached him. The Thebans, disappointed to find him alive, still refused to surrender. The young king's patience ran out. His army stormed the city, destroying it except for two things. The temple was saved to appease the gods, and the poet Pindar's home and descendants were spared because the dead poet had praised Macedonian monarchs in his odes. The other

Thebans were not so lucky. They were sold into slavery and their lands were divided among neighboring states.

Alexander dealt harshly with Thebes to satisfy his fiercer allies and to frighten the rest of Greece into submission. The news traveled fast. The Arcadians, who had been marching to the Thebans' aid, executed their leaders and went home. Athens hurriedly sent ten ambassadors to congratulate Alexander on his safe return from the north. Nonetheless, his allies were troubled. Never before had one Greek power so destroyed another's home. If this could happen to Thebes, which of them might be next? The act cost Alexander much of the diplomatic trust Philip had established.

The Greeks were still prepared, however, to follow Alexander into Asia. Their mistrust of him was nothing compared to their hatred for the Persians. This hatred sprang from bitter memories of Persian aggressions and deceit.

The Persian Empire was the most powerful empire the Near East had ever known. It stretched from India to Asia Minor, north to the Caspian Sea, and south to Egypt and the borders of Arabia. Cyrus I had founded it in 552 B.C. His conquests were strengthened and enlarged by his successor, Darius I. Darius divided the empire into twenty provinces, each controlled by a governor. Instead of crushing the conquered peoples, Darius let them keep their local customs, religions, and languages. This made Persian rule easier for them to accept. Darius did not want revolt — he wanted money. And taxes were much simpler to collect in peacetime.

As the Persians moved west, they soon encountered the Greeks. A crucial battle between them was fought at

Marathon in 490 B.C., a battle in which the Greeks triumphed. A messenger ran over twenty-two miles to deliver news of the victory. After gasping out the glad tidings, he fell down and died. His feat lived on, giving both a name and an approximate distance to the marathon run still held today.

Despite the setback at Marathon the Persians were not discouraged for long. The last of their great rulers, Xerxes, inherited a stable realm from Darius, but like most conquerors, he was not looking for stability. Again the Persians attacked the Greeks. This time they managed to reach Athens. In 480 B.C., the city was looted and burned. But a few months afterward, the Athenian fleet defeated the Persians in a huge sea battle. Twenty more years passed, though, before the Persians halted their western advance.

Sixty years later, after periods of peace and war in Greece, the Persians attacked again. This time they had Sparta as an ally, and the victory was theirs. In a treaty of 386 B.C., Sparta became the leader of Greece and both the Asiatic Greek cities and Cyprus became Persian territories. Since then the Persians had been content to stir rivalries among the city-states, prompting them to fight with one another. The Persian strategy was simple: while Greeks fought Greeks, they would not fight Persians, too.

But the triumphs of Philip and Alexander had changed the situation. The Persians also had changed. Their army in the winter of 334 B.C. was not the mighty one Xerxes had once led. It cast as large a shadow perhaps, but the shadow was not as dark as before. The current emperor, Darius III, had far greater resources in men and materials than the Greeks did, but the empire had weakened steadily under decades of laziness. The Persians had spent the time enjoying their riches. Darius did not immediately gather troops to repel the Greek invaders. Persian preparations were sluggish. Unlike the Greeks, they had no wrongs to avenge. Persian families and homes had not been threatened in over ten generations.

Alexander's position was much less secure. One reason he began the Persian campaign so quickly was to capture the fabled Persian wealth. He needed it to erase the large debt he and Philip had accumulated. As it was, Alexander put up his own lands as collateral to secure the funds to begin the invasion. This does not mean a rich Alexander would have stayed home. War and glory were his passions, and nowhere would war be more glorious than against the Persians.

Before Alexander left Greece, he reportedly went to the oracle at Delphi. The oracle was a woman who interpreted the will of the god Apollo through prophecies. Alexander wanted to know Apollo's opinion of the coming war. The oracle declared, however, that the god could not be approached at that time. Alexander was not in the mood to wait. Dragging the priestess by the hair, he pulled her to the altar. "My son," she told him, "you are invincible." Whether she spoke from prophecy or simply to get Alexander out of her hair is not known. At least he was satisfied. He left Delphi without waiting to hear what, if anything, Apollo had to say.

His affairs in order, Alexander led the army from Pella in midspring. Philip's trusted general Antipater was left behind with thirteen thousand soldiers to maintain control of Greece.

Alexander took twenty days to cross the three hundred miles to the Dardanelles. For thirty-five thousand people to march fifteen miles a day for almost three weeks was a considerable feat. Throughout his campaigns, Alexander's lightning-fast marches helped him on many occasions.

Most of the army was infantry, with a few thousand cavalry. About half the force were Macedonians; the others were Thessalians, southern Greeks, and groups from various conquered lands. The army, though, was not made up of warriors alone. The many siege engineers could build rolling towers for climbing enemy walls, catapults that discharged either arrows or boulders, and floating bridges for crossing treacherous rivers. The surveying corps kept track

Two bronze helmets. The first is of the so-called Thracian type, which was worn by Macedonian infantry troops at the time of Alexander the Great. The second is of the Chalkidian type, which protected the sides of the wearer's head.

of each day's march and collected information on local geography. Botanists and biologists studied plants and animals. And to record these events, scribes were employed to keep an official journal. Alexander wasn't going to leave his place in history to chance.

All of these people crossed the Dardanelles together. Alexander's first action in Asia was to visit Troy, the place where the war described in the *Iliad* was fought. There, he and his friend Hephaestion honored the fallen heroes of that ancient war, especially Achilles. Alexander and Hephaestion had an intimate friendship, much like Achilles had enjoyed with his friend Patroclus. As was the custom, Alexander ran naked around Achilles' gravestone, crowning it

A head of Hephaestion, Alexander's closest companion, who died during the last expeditions in the East. While there are many portraits of Alexander, ones of Hephaestion have been harder to isolate.

with flowers. Hephaestion did the same thing at Patroclus' grave. Alexander also supposedly exchanged his shield for one remaining from the Trojan War. This gesture was meant to link his future efforts with the Greeks' first known invasion of Asia.

Returning to the army, Alexander began a two-day journey inland to the Granicus River. The Persians awaited him on the other side. Darius had no master strategy to resist Alexander; his army had been gathered from the Persian forces nearby. Among the Persian generals was Memnon, a commander of Greek mercenaries. These soldiers-for-hire fought for money, not patriotism. Memnon knew that the Greek army planned to live off the land it conquered, because Alexander had no other way of supplying his troops. Memnon therefore suggested falling back before the Greek advance, and destroying or removing all supplies the Greeks would need. This strategy might well have stopped Alexander before he had truly started. But the Persians rejected the notion. It would have meant betraying their subjects. They even accused Memnon of trying to prolong the war for his own gain. Besides, what glory was there in retreat? It would be better to end the Greek threat at once.

Meanwhile, Alexander was advised by his generals to be cautious about crossing the river. If his troops broke ranks in the water, they would be very vulnerable to a Persian attack on the opposite bank. Alexander had more faith in his army, especially his phalanxes. Battles had customarily been decided in a hodge-podge of hand-to-hand combat. The phalanxes worked as a unit. Even in the midst of battle they could change their shape and direction on command. With the cavalry fanning out on both sides of them, the phalanxes were extremely powerful.

Taking his place in front of his troops, Alexander rode into the river on Bucephalus. He would send no soldier where he feared to go himself. And he did not fear to fight a Persian force no bigger than his own.

In the first charge, the Greek generals' caution seemingly was justified. Alexander led an attack into the middle of the Persians, driving back those in front of him, yet cutting himself off from much support. He made a natural target under his white plumes and bright armor. Persian cavalrymen swarmed around him. While he dealt with two of them, a third almost cut him down. He was saved at the last moment by his friend Cleitus, who killed the attacker. Enough of the phalanxes had now crossed the river to begin turning the momentum of battle. The Greeks were prepared for a lengthy attack, having faced similar ones in the past. The Persians were not. As the charge broke through their lines, they finally panicked and ran away.

To encourage his soldiers, Alexander was generous with the captured goods. He enriched the survivors, buried the Greek casualties in magnificent ceremonies, and freed their families from all taxes and personal services in their lifetimes. Alexander understood the value of morale. With such rewards, the army was eager to fight on.

But there was no more fighting at first. For one thing, most of the Persian army was still a thousand miles away. For another, the nearby cities were largely settled by Greeks. They welcomed Alexander as a liberator. Many cities in Asia Minor were happy to throw off Persian rule, especially once Alexander began setting up democracies in its place. He treated those who surrendered with courtesy and respect, prompting more surrenders in turn. Alexander had learned well from Philip's example. Where diplomacy could achieve a certain gain, there was no need for battle. And unlike so many conquerors before and after him, who mindlessly destroyed the people they defeated, Alexander left those he vanquished largely undisturbed. He wanted their support. Senseless death and destruction had no part in his plans.

Alexander showed similar foresight in handling Memnon's captured lands. The Greeks considered Memnon a traitor. They had not yet been able to kill him, but destroying his lands seemed like the next best thing. Alexander forebade this. He respected Memnon, and hoped to win the mercenary over to the Greek cause. Treating Memnon's lands gently was a step in this direction. At the very least, it would make the Persians suspicious: how could they trust an ally whose lands were treated so carefully by Alexander?

The conquest of Asia Minor continued through all of 334 B.C. Miletus was taken through a fierce assault, as was Caria. The rest of the campaign was mostly a combination of sieges and surrenders.

The land battles were not matched by ones at sea, however. Alexander had not ordered any naval conflicts because he knew the Persian sea forces were stronger than his. His general Parmenion still advised an attack. He thought the Greeks had nothing to lose in trying.

Alexander disagreed. He saw no reason to throw away

sailors and ships on a doomed mission. And even justifiable defeats were bad for morale. Besides, he no longer needed ships to gain a foothold in Asia. The Persian navy remained a threat to Greece and his conquests, but Alexander had a plan to deal with it. If the Greeks could capture the whole eastern Mediterranean coast, the Persian navy would be at their mercy. Even a mighty fleet would be helpless without ports to dock at for new supplies.

The winter of 333 B.C. saw Alexander at Gordium in Phrygia. The care Alexander showed his men was a mark of his leadership, and he displayed it now. Knowing that many of his soldiers had gotten married just before leaving Macedonia, he sent them home to their wives till spring. Not surprisingly, his popularity soared. Alexander was steadily building a bond between himself and his men that would be invaluable in the coming years.

Unlike many of his men, Alexander remained in Gordium, where he encountered the famous Gordian Knot. This knot held together the yoke and pole of an ancient wagon. Neither the beginning nor the end of the knot was visible. According to legend, whoever could loosen the knot would someday rule Asia. Alexander was planning to rule Asia, so naturally he gave the knot his attention.

Two stories have survived about what happened next. One is that Alexander slid the yoke out of the knot, revealing hidden ends easy to untie. The other is that the knot stumped him, so he cut it with his sword, loosening it permanently. Both explanations suit his nature. He was ingenious enough to have removed the yoke, which nobody had ever thought of doing before. Then again, he was never shy about using his sword. Both stories agree that a thunderstorm raged during the event. Alexander took this as a sign that the gods were heralding the occasion.

While Alexander enjoyed his good fortune, the Persians suffered a loss. After the Granicus River defeat, the Persian emperor Darius had put Memnon in charge of his forces. The clever Greek had devised several strategies, including a plan for attacking Greece itself. If he could stir up enough trouble there, Alexander would have to return home to deal with it. Unfortunately for the Persians, Memnon fell ill and died before the plan was settled. Without him, the Persians lacked a general who truly understood the ways of the enemy.

Spring and fresh troops arrived together. Alexander began a march inland, taking several more cities. Spring came to the Persians, too. And now that Alexander had left the coast, their still strong fleet recaptured some territory. The problem for Alexander was that not even he could be in two places at once. Clearly the Persian fleet would have to be neutralized before Alexander advanced too far from the Mediterranean.

But before he could do much about it, another problem developed. After a particularly long and dry march, Alexander had gone swimming in a bitterly cold river. Now a fever had set in. The campaign came to a halt while his doctors tried to cure him. None of their efforts succeeded. The army waited anxiously. Though the soldiers were a powerful force in themselves, it was Alexander who supplied the crucial spark of leadership. Without him, the fragile Greek union would have dissolved.

Fortunately a recent arrival in camp, Philip the Arcananian, began treating Alexander. He made Alexander a new medicine to drink. Just as the preparations were done, Alexander received a note from Parmenion. It accused Philip of being a Persian spy. Supposedly he had been bribed by Darius to kill Alexander. If this were true, then the medicine Alexander was about to drink must be poisonous. But Alexander considered Philip a friend. The king took the potion and handed Philip the letter. While Alexander drank, Philip read the note in outrage, protesting his innocence. It wasn't necessary. Alexander had gambled on his intuition about people. And his faith in Philip was rewarded, for the doctor cured him.

While the campaign had stalled during Alexander's illness, Darius had been gathering his forces at the Euphrates River. Now the Persians marched to confront the Macedonian upstart. But because of faulty communications and scouting, a strange thing happened. The two armies passed each other on opposite sides of a mountain at night. When Alexander discovered this he turned around. Darius and sixty thousand Persian troops were waiting for him. For hours Alexander advanced slowly, hoping the Persians would make an ill-conceived attack. Darius simply waited. When the battle came, the two cavalries engaged each other furiously. Persian archers sent a hail of arrows raining down on the Greek phalanxes. In a surprise move, Alexander ordered the phalanxes forward. This meant running through a shower of arrows. The phalanxes obeyed, and the astonished archers fell back in amazement. As the fight continued, Darius himself felt threatened by the Greek advance. He turned and fled. This one act made the difference.

Clay bowl showing a battle scene between the Greeks and the Persians. Probably made in the late second–early first century B.C.

The Persian cavalry, seeing their emperor's flight, began to retreat. The other Persians soon followed their lead. Victory went to the Greeks.

Darius had fled so hastily that his tents and family were left behind. His captured belongings gave Alexander his first taste of the splendor the Persian emperors enjoyed. Darius did not travel lightly. When he moved about, he carried a small city of nobles, servants, and entertainers with him. War for Darius was partly like a country outing.

In his treatment of Darius' family, Alexander showed a gentleness that marked his treatment of women. This was very unusual in a period when most conquerors treated women like any other captured property. In contrast, Alexander was polite and generous to Darius' wife, mother, and two daughters, all of whom probably feared for their lives. Who knows what horrid tales they had heard about this Macedonian rabble-rouser? Alexander put them at ease. He ordered that they should continue receiving the care and respect they were accustomed to getting. This was no small favor. It allowed them greater luxuries than Alexander himself enjoyed.

Following the victory, Alexander returned to the Mediterranean coast. With every step, the Persian fleet was more isolated from its bases. The captured cities also supplied Alexander with a growing number of ships. Darius now wrote to Alexander, offering peace and a ransom for his family. Alexander refused the terms. He would accept only unconditional surrender from the Persians. In Darius' eyes, a few Greek victories had not given them that complete a triumph. So the fighting went on.

Alexander soon faced the most difficult siege he ever undertook. It involved the Phoenician city of Tyre. Tyre had a proud and rich heritage stretching back over a thousand years, and it was stubbornly independent. Built on an island half a mile from shore, Tyre could not be attacked from the coast. And its high walls made a naval assault impractical, even assuming Alexander had the necessary ships. Two centuries earlier, the mighty Babylonian king Nebuchadnezzar had besieged Tyre for thirteen years without success. What hope did Alexander have of doing better?

Little hope, if he used the Babylonian methods. He couldn't surround the city any more effectively than they had, and even if he could, he didn't have thirteen years to wait out a siege. The Persians were threatening his forces on too many fronts.

To defeat Tyre, Alexander would have to enter the city. To do that, he would have to bring down the walls. Yet no catapulted boulders or battering rams could reach out half a mile from shore. Alexander solved the problem with a bold stroke of engineering. He began building a causeway, a raised road jutting out from the beach toward Tyre.

Naturally, the Phoenicians tried to stop him. They deliberately set ships on fire and aimed them at the construction. The incomplete causeway was destroyed. Alexander answered by building another, wider one. He also used his newly taken ships to create a blockade around the island. This hindered any further interference.

The second causeway took seven months to complete, an eternity for the impatient Alexander. But when it was done, the attack began. The walls were demolished and the Greeks won the fierce battle that followed. Many people were killed and the surviving women and children were sold into slavery. When Alexander's enemies surrendered or fought quickly and bravely, he was lenient and forgiving. But if, as with Thebes and now Tyre, his foes were exasperating, he was decidedly brutal.

The significance of Tyre's fall exceeded its value as a trade center or a naval base. Tyre was the seat of Phoenician power, and Phoenician sailors manned the Persian fleet. These sailors were not stupid. They could see the balance of power shifting in the Middle East. It would be wise for them to join the winning side. As the Phoenicians were gradually won over, the Persian naval threat in the Mediterranean disappeared.

During the siege of Tyre, Darius had sent Alexander another proposal. This one greatly sweetened his request for peace. A staggering amount of gold was offered for the return of his family. In addition, he also offered Alexander his daughter in marriage and all the lands west of the Euphrates River. It seemed like a tempting bid, and the general Parmenion advised Alexander to take it.

"I would accept," he wrote the king, "were I Alexander."

"So would I," was Alexander's reply, "were I Parmenion." Darius was in no position, thought Alexander, to give away something he would soon lose anyway. With such confidence, the proposal was refused.

After Tyre, the city of Gaza also contested the Greek advance. Engineers reported that because the city was built on a large mound surrounded by deep sand, the siege machines could not reach the walls. As Alexander had already showed at Tyre, nothing spurred him on like doing what seemed impossible. And Gaza was important to take, being the last stronghold between the Greek forces and Egypt.

So once again the engineers went to work. They first built a giant ramp up to the walls for the siege machines to roll on. The city's defenders, however, managed to set fire to these machines and even pushed many of them off the ramp itself. In a new strategy, Alexander had an elevated ring built around the city. Other siege machines were placed upon it and used to batter the walls.

This was still not enough. Alexander finally sent his miners to dig under the walls themselves. To protect the working soldiers, huge towers covered with layers of animal skins were rolled over their heads. It wasn't easy to dig while worrying about being shot in the back with an arrow, but the miners did their best. The walls weakened, finally falling under the combined assault. Another frenzied battle ended with another Greek victory.

Egypt was next. The Persian governor there had kept track of Alexander's progress. A practical man, he surrendered without a fight. The Egyptians themselves rejoiced at Alexander's arrival in 332 B.C. They had hated Persian rule. Alexander traveled to Memphis, where he sacrificed to the Egyptian gods and was crowned as a pharaoh.

Alexander did not show respect to local religions merely to be polite. He hoped to get the priests to support him. He knew that priests could be powerful friends or enemies because of their influence over the people. For their part, the priests aided Alexander because he allowed them to keep their power.

By this time, Alexander was quite pleased with his success. He founded the city of Alexandria in his own honor where the Nile River met the Mediterranean. Alexandria was planned with straight streets in an organized pattern, unlike the twisting, winding avenues of other ancient cities. Alexander marked out the city's design himself, reportedly using trails of grain because no chalk was available. Birds flew down to eat the grain, lucky for them perhaps, but very likely a bad omen. Alexander's imaginative soothsayers dispelled the king's worries. They told him this event meant the city would be a source of food for many people, hence a prosperous place.

Satisfied on this point, Alexander made a difficult journey into Libya to visit the famous oracle of Ammon at Siwah. The legendary heroes Perseus and Heracles had reputedly taken the same trip. Alexander could do no less. Unlike his experience at Delphi, this oracle welcomed his arrival. He and the oracle met privately, and he told no one what was said between them. He was very open, however, about being happy with the news. Rumor had it that the oracle told Alexander he was the son of a god. Whether this happened or not, Alexander's interest in his divine ancestry increased from that journey onward. Alexander did not yet think himself a god. Probably he saw his supposed divinity as a way of impressing his subjects. As time passed, it became a way of impressing himself.

In the spring of 331 B.C., Alexander left Egypt and returned to Syria. In July, he entered Mesopotamia and crossed the Euphrates River. Already he had come farther than any Greek leader before him. The full might of the Persian Empire was now massed for battle on the plain of Gaugamela near Arbela. It was not, however, a force of hundreds of thousands, as later ancient historians reported. Darius had far more cavalry than Alexander, but also far less infantry. In pulling representatives from all parts of the empire, Darius even had elephants from India. The heart of the Persian strength, though, was its chariot force. These chariots were deadly to foot soldiers in their path, if awkward to maneuver. Whatever the actual size of the Persian army, it is safe to assume that the Greeks were distinctly outnumbered.

Knowing the need for each man to excel, Alexander gave his troops a stirring speech. He cited their earlier bravery, pointing up their strengths and the Persians' weaknesses. Once they were suitably roused, he retired to confer with his generals. They advised him to lead a surprise attack at night. The darkness and confusion might aid their smaller numbers.

Alexander refused the suggestion. "I will not steal a victory," he replied. He would not give Darius any pos-

44

sible excuses for defeat. Most likely he also realized that darkness could confuse Greeks as well as Persians. This decision worked nicely in his favor. The Persians had reasoned out the Greek position. A night attack made sense to them, and they waited for it in readiness. They had not reckoned with Alexander's ego. He soundly slept the night away.

In fact, he slept late. It was midmorning before the battle began. Regiments of cavalry met first, stirring up the dust of the dry plain. Then the powerful Persian chariots rumbled forward. Alexander had known the phalanxes could not meet them head on, so he had ordered the men to part ranks to let the chariots go by. The charioteers could not turn or stop fast enough to keep the phalanxes in front of them. Once the chariots had passed, the phalanxes attacked them from the sides and rear. The charioteers never got a chance for a second charge.

On other parts of the plain the Persians were doing better. The Macedonian cavalry was sorely pressed and Alexander sent them some reinforcements. Darius then made the mistake of committing too much of his strength to this encounter. It opened up a gap through which Alexander could engage Darius himself. Alexander lost no time attempting it. Spurring Bucephalus forward, he led the thrust at the emperor. Darius did not answer it — he fled again. And once more, the Persian army followed his lead. Its generals lost interest in fighting for an emperor who would not stand by them. Resistance soon collapsed, though the fighting continued for hours. For Alexander, though, victory was incomplete without the capture of Darius. After the battle ended, he hotly pursued the

Persian emperor. But it was then too late to catch him.

This second decisive triumph broke the Persian Empire wide open. The cities of Babylon and Susa both surrendered to Alexander. He spent the following winter in Babylon, a majestic city though power had long since passed from it. The immense outer walls were reportedly three hundred feet high. Nebuchadnezzar's palace, which was several centuries old, had six hundred rooms. The Hanging Gardens there were later acclaimed one of the Seven Wonders of the Ancient World. Babylon had once been a great trade center, and Alexander saw that it could be again. He began plans to enlarge the harbor.

East met West in Babylon as they were beginning to meet in Alexander's mind. For now, this was only evident in a political decision. Instead of simply replacing the Persian governor, Alexander added a Macedonian commander to rule with him.

From Babylon, Alexander went to Susa, the capital of Persia, where he left Darius' family. He then started for Persepolis, subduing some rebellious tribes along the way. In the narrow mountain passes, however, he met more organized resistance. The governor of Persia, at the head of forty thousand men, ambushed the Greeks. Amid heavy casualties, the retreat was sounded. Alexander did not repeat his mistake. With the help of a native guide, he sent some troops to circle behind the enemy during the night. In the subsequent battle, the Greeks attacked from two sides. The Persians were caught in a trap, and few of them lived to remember it.

Alexander faced no further opposition in Persia. On reaching Persepolis, ritual center of the Persian Empire, the

Greeks held a great celebration. They had a lot to celebrate. Not only had they unseated the Persian emperor, but the wealth found in Persepolis was overwhelming. During the festivities, the palace of Xerxes was burned, a late revenge for his invasion of Greece and the burning of Athens. No effort was made to preserve any rugs, tapestries or other Persian artifacts in the palace, and they were all destroyed in the blaze. The fire also served to cripple Persepolis as the potential center for any future rebellion.

The destruction of Xerxes' palace marked the end of the Greek effort to avenge the many years of Persian war and mischief. And once Alexander learned that Darius no longer commanded an army, changes were made. Until now, Alexander had been acting as the commander of the League of Corinth, representing all of its members. His mission for the League was over. He therefore dismissed the League troops. Those who wished to return home would return there as rich men. Those who wanted to fight on were invited to enlist in the remaining Macedonian-based army. There they would serve Alexander alone in his role as king of Macedonia, pharaoh of Egypt, and emperor of Persia.

When this transition was accomplished, Alexander led his army eastward in pursuit of Darius. The defeated emperor had taken refuge with Bessus, the governor of Bactria. Alexander sped after them. News reached him that Bessus had betrayed Darius, and held him prisoner. Alexander chased the fugitives without stopping for two days and nights. But he found Darius too late — the last of the Persian emperors was discovered dead in the wilderness, betrayed by Bessus, the last of his followers.

3

As the newly crowned Persian emperor, Alexander reached heights undreamed of by any Greek leader before him. Yet his consuming ambition was still not satisfied. The eastern half of the Persian Empire had not been subdued, and the traitor Bessus remained free. He had raised an army in Afghanistan, and begun calling himself king of Persia. He was not a grave threat to Alexander, but the new emperor had never been one to refuse a challenge.

After quashing a southern revolt, Alexander marched toward Afghanistan, planning to confront Bessus. Alexander met little resistance along the way. The natives generally surrendered to him, as much in surprise at finding him in their rugged terrain as for any other reason. In each conquered city, Alexander left a Persian in political power, while Macedonians kept charge of the treasury and the local garrison of soldiers.

This behavior upset the Macedonians. Unrest had lately entered their ranks. They had always been the elite of Alexander's fighting force, and Macedonian generals had been his closest advisers. He was one of them, they thought. But now Alexander had started wearing Persian clothing and introducing Persian customs into his court. Several Persians had become his friends. The Macedonians shook their heads at this. Foreigners had no business meddling in the affairs of their conquerors. They should be treated like slaves. Instead, these former enemies had been placed among the Macedonian officers. Alexander obviously did not share their views. He took on Persian customs partly because he liked them and partly to match the image the Persians expected of their emperor. The Macedonians could grumble all they wanted. He wouldn't change his mind.

Still, as the gap between them widened, Alexander became more and more distrustful of his own people. He drank a great deal at banquets, and listened increasingly to flatterers. His suspicions focused on anyone with a large following in the army.

Parmenion's son Philotas was one prominent officer who had gained much independent stature. Philotas enjoyed his fame and he made no secret of this. Parmenion had warned him in vain that "to be not quite so great would be better." He meant it would be safer. The old general had not forgotten how ruthless Alexander could be with a rival.

Philotas made matters worse by criticizing Alexander's new Persian habits. Soon thereafter, he was found guilty of knowing about a plot against Alexander, but not reporting it. Whether Philotas had actually committed treason or had just been foolish, Alexander was in no mood to be merciful. Philotas was put to death. Macedonian law also allowed for a traitor's relatives to be executed. It was a coarse way of cleaning up loose ends. Unsure of how his general Parmenion would react to his son's death, Alexander used this law to have Parmenion killed. The Macedonians did not protest openly at these actions, but the grumblings continued.

These troubles did not interfere, however, with Alexander's military performance. His ability to lead his army through all kinds of territory was extraordinary. Afghanistan was a long way from Greece, yet the army marched over rugged mountains and arid plains, defeating tribes on their native terrain. In December of 330 B.C., Alexander reached the Kabul valley. Amid the snow and bitter cold, even he would not attempt to cross the Hindu Kush, an eleven-thousand-foot-high mountain range. He waited till spring, and that the soldiers managed it even then was incredible.

The next two years were spent hunting Bessus and his allies through the wilderness. This was a dismal time for the army, a series of quick marches and quicker battles, all for little obvious gain. The driving force behind their campaigns had left them at Persepolis. The fighting now was more like Alexander's personal war, a war his army found increasingly hard to justify to themselves.

Bessus was finally captured, the traitor betrayed by his former allies. He was publicly exhibited, bound and naked, before being sent back to the western Persian city of Ecbatana for execution. His death did not end the hostilities in eastern Persia. Several major rebel leaders remained at large, and Alexander was determined to track them down.

One of these leaders, Oxyartes, had his stronghold at a

natural fortress called Sogdiana Rock. Alexander's army reached its base and he demanded its surrender. The enemy sentries looked down from the sheer cliffs and laughed. "Go find soldiers with wings," they were said to have taunted him.

Alexander went to less trouble. He offered rich prizes to the first dozen men to reach the top of the fortress. That night, three hundred soldiers scaled the cliffs. Foot by foot, they chipped holes for pegs and climbed up on them. The sentries were overpowered, and Macedonians swarmed through the fortress. The surprised Sogdians surrendered.

Among them was Oxyartes' daughter Roxane. Her youth and beauty appealed to Alexander, and he knew the wisdom of winning Oxyartes' willing support. A marriage was soon arranged. Though Oxyartes had been a determined foe, he now served under his son-in-law.

By the end of 328 B.C., the eastern part of the empire had been subdued, though at great cost in men and morale. Alexander almost always drank heavily at meals, and his temper was perilously short. He was surrounded by flatterers who compared him with the gods. Alexander enjoyed the comparison and encouraged it.

The change in him both saddened and outraged his old friends, men who had known him since his youth. One of them was Cleitus, who had saved Alexander's life at the Granicus River. Cleitus spoke his mind at a banquet, scolding Alexander for assuming Persian and godlike ways. Most likely the wine had loosened his tongue. Stung by the criticism, Alexander demanded his sword. One of his servants had already removed it. Mutual friends now tried to intercede, but Cleitus' voice would not be stilled. Alexander then lost all control. He grabbed a guard's spear, and a moment later Cleitus was dead.

The murder finally brought Alexander to his senses. Overcome with remorse, he collapsed at his friend's side. For three days he refused to eat or even leave his tent. The army had been shocked by the murder, but they feared now to lose Alexander as well as Cleitus. And the king's repentance had moved them. Therefore they passed a decree convicting Cleitus of treason, even though he was already dead. Their decree gave Alexander a legal excuse for his action.

The army's decree, however legal, could not erase the murder from the memories of Alexander's officers. They became more reluctant than ever to disagree with him. Alexander took this as a sign of his own wisdom. His ego was further inflated by the Persians' habit of bowing — sometimes even groveling — before him. In its most extreme form, this meant slithering on the ground like a snake. The Macedonians did not share such traditions about their rulers. They held that the king was a leader chosen by his equals, not someone who was superior to them. So, they balked at following the Persian example. Alexander wanted them to make at least a simple bow in his presence. But the Macedonians were stiff-necked where their principles were concerned. Such gestures were the habits of slaves, not free men. In fact, Antipater's son, Cassander, laughed aloud the first time he saw Persians prostrating themselves before Alexander. He should have kept quiet. Alexander grabbed him by the hair and dashed his head against a wall. Cassander survived, but years after Alexander's death, when Cassander was king of Macedonia, he still shuddered when passing statues of Alexander.

Alexander soon stopped trying to make his men bow to him — it was causing laughter, not respect. He did not, however, abandon his quest for more territory. The army fought its way all over the landscape of modern Pakistan, leaving behind five new cities, each named Alexandria. No pocket of resistance was too small for Alexander to crush. He tracked them down relentlessly. Conquest had ceased to be a means to an end. It had become an end in itself.

It had been Alexander's plan for some time to attack India, and in the summer of 327 B.C., he embarked on this campaign. His first move was to deal with the large amount of baggage the army was carting around. No longer was this the trim fighting force that had crossed the Dardanelles into Asia. It was loaded down with the spoils of war. Alexander soon saw that the stuffed wagons and burdened pack animals would be a hindrance in the months ahead. In another of his dramatic strokes, Alexander set his own wagon on fire, encouraging others to do the same to theirs. No doubt some soldiers saw their dreams of wealth as well as their baggage going up in smoke. Loyally, though, the army followed Alexander's example.

The India that Alexander was invading was far bigger than he knew. Greek geography was sketchy about that part of the world. Alexander thought he was close to the far edge of Asia; he actually had only passed about half way across it.

His ignorance, though, did not affect the first part of the campaign. The army made rapid progress to the Indus River, where they were met by the rajah Ambhi. This was a friendly meeting. The rajah gave them troops, elephants, and a huge gift of livestock. The livestock at least were welcomed hungrily by the army. Ambhi's generosity was not without reason. He wanted to enlist Alexander's aid against another rajah, Porus. Alexander was glad to oblige.

Porus was well prepared for his coming. He waited on the far side of the Hydapses River with thirty-five thousand troops and two hundred elephants. This was a different problem from the one Alexander had faced at the Granicus River years before. Then he had attacked from the water despite the tactical disadvantage. But there were no elephants at the Granicus. Elephants frightened horses that had never seen them before. If the Greeks crossed the river openly, the elephants on the other side would make their horses bolt. And on tightly packed boats, frightened horses would lead to disaster.

Therefore, Alexander waited, pretending to start across the river several times to keep Porus guessing. He ordered so much movement up and down miles of riverbank that Porus' scouts grew to expect it. Not until a night thunderstorm hid his efforts did he attempt a crossing with some of his troops. The thunderstorm was almost as dangerous as the elephants, the wind and rain rocking the boats and hindering communications. Alexander had wisely made the crossing many miles from Porus' camp. When the movement was discovered, Porus could not send much of a force to meet it. If he did, the rest of the Macedonian and Indian allies would cross at once. Alexander thus reached the other side safely, where he defeated the troops Porus had sent to greet him. Porus' gamble had lost. He now had to attack Alexander directly. While he did so, the rest of Alexander's army crossed the river.

A long battle followed. The Indians were fine warriors, brave and well trained. They did not give ground easily. Porus used his elephants with great effect, breaking through the Greek lines again and again. He sat calmly astride one of them, like a giant watching ants scurry at his feet. The battle did not turn decisively until the Macedonian cavalry pushed the Indian horsemen back into their own ranks. The hard-pressed cavalry crowded their own elephants. Once bunched together, the elephants panicked, rampaging among Porus' own troops. The Indians soon retreated in disorder.

The defeated Porus was brought before Alexander. The Indian rajah had not fled like Darius. He was a brave man, a good soldier, and a proud monarch. Alexander respected him for this.

He asked Porus how he should be treated.

Porus answered, "As a king."

He was asked to elaborate and replied with the same words, stating that they said everything.

Alexander was even more impressed than before. What-

A silver coin showing Alexander on horseback attacking Porus, who is seated on a retreating elephant.

ever fate Porus envisioned, he must have been surprised. For Alexander made him the ruler of a province even larger than the area he had governed before.

One notable casualty of this battle was Alexander's horse, Bucephalus. In later years, Alexander had spared his steed any riding except for the main charge into battle. The two had been companions for twenty years. Now old age and weariness had taken their final toll, and the horse died. Alexander mourned the loss as he would have mourned the death of any other close friend. He even built a memorial city, Bucephala, before continuing the campaign.

Alexander spent the next few months putting down small rebellions. He had become somewhat like a bull that will charge at anything red: Alexander charged any people who wished to stay independent. Once they were defeated, however, he usually gave them independent status under his overall rule. The battles thus had little meaning to the army. The soldiers also realized that while they had fought in eastern Persia to protect western Persia, India had no such strategic value. The soldiers were tired after their difficult victory over Porus, and they felt they had little to show for it. They had also heard discouraging tales about armies four and five times their size still waiting for them farther along. The heavy rains of the Indian monsoon season washed away any remaining enthusiasm.

The army's reluctance to go on surprised Alexander. He tried to rally his officer's spirits as he had in the past. They had already conquered so many places — only a few more, and all of Asia would be theirs.

The soldiers were not convinced. One of their generals, Coenus, acted as the army's spokesman. In an emotional speech, he begged Alexander to turn back.

The king was not pleased. He sulked in his tent for three days mulling over the decision. Personally, of course, he wished to go on. But he realized that, even if the army followed his lead, a reluctant army would fight poorly. Bowing to the circumstances, Alexander gave in. The army rejoiced.

It was November, 326 B.C., when Alexander finally halted his eastern advance. Heading for home, though, did not mean retracing his steps. The army went south on a nine-month river journey to the Indian Ocean. Along the way, Alexander went looking for trouble wherever he could find it. He found plenty with a tribe called the Malloi.

Their first confrontation came in a remote city. The Malloi assumed Alexander would not attempt the difficult journey to reach it. They were wrong. He did so precisely because the trip was difficult. The unprepared city was soon taken, as were several others.

But the greatest city of the Malloi still remained. There they were prepared for Alexander. The outer town fell before the Greeks, but the inner fortress held. Determined to breach it, Alexander impulsively led a small assault over the walls. Only a few bodyguards were with him. Heavily outnumbered, they fought for their lives.

When relief reached them, Alexander had already been badly wounded. An arrow was lodged in his chest. Rumors of Alexander's death spread throughout the army, though he still lived. His recovery, however, was slow and painful.

With the return of his health, the Malloi surrendered.

When Alexander reached the ocean, some of his soldiers were sent by ship to explore the Persian Gulf. Alexander wished for evidence of a sea route between Persia and India. The rest of the army marched overland with him. The worst part of the trek was an eleven-hundred-mile stretch through the desert. Alexander knew of its hardships, but he wanted to be the first commander to bring an army across it in orderly fashion.

The fashion was not so orderly. The soldiers trudged slowly through the rippling dunes. In the shade of dry bushes lurked poisonous snakes; food and water ran short. Alexander expected to meet up with his fleet and fresh supplies along the coast, but the fleet was delayed by bad weather. Faced with sitting and starving or marching on, the army returned to the desert. Discipline almost disappeared. Pack animals and horses were killed for food; wagons were burned for warmth during the freezing nights. The unrelenting heat during the day claimed many lives, and then, ironically, flash floods from storms in the mountains caused deaths as well. Alexander suffered no less than his men. In the middle of a dry march, scouts found enough water to fill one helmet. They brought it to Alexander. He thanked them and poured the water into the sand. The king would not drink while his army went thirsty. This gesture boosted his soldiers' flagging spirits. They marched on.

After sixty days, the army finally reached the city of Pura. Alexander's eastern campaign was over. Three-fourths of the original army had died on the Indian expedition, many of them during the hazardous trip back.

There is no record of Alexander ever questioning whether the campaign was worth it. He was too busy settling more practical matters. Many leaders he had left behind had abused their power, thinking Alexander would never return. Their abuses had fueled discontent throughout the empire. Even in Greece, the situation was not calm. The general Antipater and Alexander's mother, Olympias, who were supposed to be ruling together, quarreled constantly.

Alexander dealt swiftly with the offenders. In the next two years, more than a third of the provincial governors were removed from office. The swift justice cut across national lines. Macedonians were treated as harshly as Persians. Several were put to death. Important military figures, guilty of extortion, were also tried and executed. Clearly, Alexander had been away too long.

While setting the empire in order, Alexander took further steps to unite Greek and Persian interests. His efforts in this area reflected his unique vision. But because it had never been tried before, few of his contemporaries understood it. Alexander was striving to combine the best of East and West, not merely impose one culture on the other. Toward that end, thirty thousand Persian boys had been receiving a Greek education. Their progress pleased him greatly. From the Persians he took his system of government, a union of provinces each with its own administration.

The most dramatic of Alexander's efforts, though, were the marriages he arranged in Susa between ten thousand of his troops and the Persian women they had met. The weddings were held in one gigantic ceremony. Even Alexander participated, taking Darius' daughter, Stateira, as his second wife. Nine thousand guests watched the event, and each of them received a gold cup from Alexander. He also gave handsome gifts to all of the newlyweds. The celebration continued for five days, with performing musicians and actors highlighting the festivities.

Before he left Susa, Alexander made a generous offer to his soldiers, hoping to heal the rift that had opened between them. He proposed to pay their debts; all they had to do was come forward and reveal what the debts were. His men hesitated, thinking it a trick to get them to betray their bad habits. Alexander mocked them for their lack of trust. Still, he amended the terms. He would pay off all their debts without recording any names. There was now no question of a trick, and the grateful soldiers settled up. This act alone cost Alexander a king's ransom, yet it could not resolve some of the dissatisfaction among his troops.

But their remaining complaints would soon be attended to. Heading for Babylon, Alexander sailed up the Tigris River to Opis. There he decreed that any sick, maimed, or older Macedonians were to be sent home. This announcement coincided with the arrival of the thirty thousand Persian boys, now ready to enter Alexander's service.

The Macedonians protested. They thought Alexander was pushing them aside, dismissing them in disgrace. It seemed like the last and greatest of the many slights they had felt. Alexander had meant no offense. But it was time for the Macedonians to realize that he considered the Persians their equals. So instead of dismissing only the sick and wounded, he threatened to replace his whole army with Persians.

A silver cup known as a *kantharos*. Vessels of this type were commonly used by Alexander.

Once again, his daring succeeded. The Macedonians pleaded for forgiveness. Alexander left them squirming for three days; then he relented. The event was marked with a celebration. Afterward, he sent ten thousand men home enriched with both money and honor.

With this crisis settled, Alexander continued his reorganization of his vast domain. His plans were interrupted, though, by an unexpected tragedy. His best friend, Hephaestion, had become ill. Against his doctor's orders he attended a banquet, where he drank too much. He became even sicker, and then died.

Alexander was inconsolable. In a blind rage, he had the attending doctor crucified. Messengers were sent throughout the empire, with orders to have Hephaestion honored everywhere as a hero. The playing of music was forbidden during the mourning period. As a final tribute, Alexander ordered the manes and tails of his horses and mules cut short, a token of respect he had given to no other fallen comrade.

Alexander's arrival in Babylon was marked by some superstitious omens that did not bode well for him. He did not let them interfere with his plans. In the fall of 324 B.C., Alexander started preparations for a fleet to explore Africa and Arabia. He also wanted to start settlements along the Persian Gulf, to begin trading with India, and to explore the Caspian Sea.

None of this was to happen under his rule. Since Hephaestion's death, Alexander had taken poor care of himself. The early months of 323 B.C. witnessed frequent drinking bouts and banquets that ran on for days. After one such affair in the beginning of June, Alexander fell sick with a fever. He continued with his regular duties for a few days, sacrificing to the gods and planning the upcoming expeditions. But the fever worsened, perhaps complicated by malaria. Alexander was now fatally ill.

When the news spread, the whole army came to file past his bed. Alexander signaled to them, waving weakly to those he knew. For ten days he lingered, feeling better at times only to suffer another relapse.

He died in mid-June, 323 B.C. His body was eventually taken to Egypt, where he was buried in a gold coffin in Alexandria.

EPILOGUE

Alexander's rise was spectacular and swift. The empire he built was held together as much by his personality as by other factors, and his death left the government in confusion. Alexander had made no preparations for the peaceful transfer of power. No one knew who should take his place, and no one had the ability and strength of character to be the obvious choice.

This did not keep some of them from trying. Alexander's pregnant wife, Roxane, sought to protect the throne for her unborn child. Toward that end, she had Alexander's Persian wife, Stateira, murdered. Meanwhile, the various generals jockeyed for position. In time, Philip Arrhidaeus, Philip's half-witted son, and Alexander IV, Alexander and Roxane's son, shared the empire. Real control, however, passed to the military.

Alexander had ruled for almost thirteen years. Within another thirteen years, both successor kings had been murdered. The Greek city-states, with generations of mistrust

This golden chest was found in the main chamber of a tomb at Vergina. The chest, unique in size and material, contained the cremated bones of a man and is decorated with the large starburst that was the emblem of the Macedonian royal line.

outweighing short years of unity, went their separate ways. Smaller provinces became independent. The bulk of the empire passed to three of Alexander's generals: Antigonus in Macedonia, Seleucus in Syria, and Ptolemy in Egypt. These three divisions maintained a balance of power until the rise of Rome over two centuries later.

That the empire could not survive his death was an ironic tribute to Alexander. His headstrong will, ingenuity, boldness, and practical nature had taken him far. Yet his genius in the craft of war was matched by his enlightened vision of different peoples sharing in a central government and one another's cultures. New cities modeled on Greek lines dotted the Asian landscape where he had passed. Babylonian science, Persian art, and Indian medicine and philosophy were brought westward to enrich Greek civilization. The Hellenistic period following Alexander's death was a time of great advancements throughout the regions he subdued, and these advances owed much to the exchange of ideas he fostered.

Alexander's fame was greater than any other leader of the pre-Roman ancient world. Throughout later periods in history, his deeds have inspired countless works of art and literature. Leaders as varied as Caesar and Napoleon looked to his campaigns for inspiration. No doubt this legacy would have pleased Alexander. His life was bound up in his search for glory, an elusive prize that had to be captured again and again. More than anything else, he was its proud, driven hunter.